ANGELS *of*

RAINBOW

BRIDGE

More Books by Dr. Ming Chee:

The Equation of Money

Money Blues to Blue Money

Being Present to Serve (Co-authored with Amina Makhdoom)

Reiki Fur Babies (Co-authored with Candy Boroditsky)

ANGELS *of*

RAINBOW BRIDGE

Life After Transition

BY: MING CHEE

ISBN: 9781688756762

Dedication

This book is dedicated to my beloved fur babies past, present and future; and to all the animals who have crossed the rainbow bridge that walked among us, loved us unconditionally, protected us and kept us company throughout good times and hard times.

There is a bridge connecting Heaven and Earth. It is called Rainbow Bridge because of its many splendid colors. Just this side of Rainbow Bridge there is a land of meadows, hills and valleys with lush, green grass.

When beloved pets die, they go to this place. There is always food and water and warm spring weather. The old and frail animals are young again. Those who are maimed are made whole again. They play all day with each other.

There is only one thing missing. They are not with their special person who loved them on earth. So, each day they run and play. Until the day comes when one suddenly stops playing and looks up!

The nose twitches. The ears are up! The eyes are staring.

And this one suddenly runs from the group. You have been seen!

And when you and your special friend meet, you take him in your arms and embrace. Your face is kissed again and again and again, and you look once more into the eyes of your trusting pet. Then you cross the Rainbow Bridge together...

... Never again to be separated.

The Rainbow Bridge, by Unknown

Contents

Foreword

Famous author James Thurber once observed that a dog's life is "spent doing pointless things that have the solemnity of inner purpose".* They look busy doing absolutely nothing. Thurber was a dog lover who was not prone to attributing human characteristics to scratching, sniffing and biting. His dog knew better. Nowadays we call it "mindfulness", staying in the moment to experience the joy of life. From Ming Chee we learn the real essence of being a dog – to love their human unconditionally with endless loyalty and boundless enthusiasm. In short, to teach us how to live and love, even when life has been harsh. Maybe, just maybe, to absorb our suffering. It's no wonder that Mr. Bojangles grieves his dog even twenty years later. When we are with our fur babies, time stops. We are enveloped in pure love. This must be what heaven feels like.

Ming Chee and her Reiki partner Candy Boroditsky, Reiki Master, animal communicator and co-founder of Reiki Fur Babies, have devoted their second careers to understanding fur babies, relieving their distress, communicating their desires in language we can understand. They have taken care of three generations of my beloved Newfoundlands in life and in spirit. While I don't profess to understanding how Reiki works, or why some people can communicate with animals while the rest of us are left wondering what *are* they thinking, I can attest to the profound relaxation and relief of pain the dogs experience when Ming and Candy are treating them.

I first found Reiki Fur Babies ten years ago when my four-year-old female Emma was broadsided by her playful two-hundred-pound brother and was walking three-legged as a result.** Of course it was Saturday night, when else do these things occur! I called them and after twenty minutes, both dogs went into a deep sleep for hours. When they awoke, my girl was weight bearing with a minor limp that resolved the next day. I was so grateful for her improvement. But what came next was astonishing. Emma said, "*Boys are so dumb, do I* *look like a pillow?"* She also appreciated the angels, but wasn't overly impressed, in her own words, *"The angels are here to love and protect Emma. Emma feels the love. Emma thinks the angels need to work on the 'protect' part."*

Thus, began ten years of talking with Newfies, seven of them, in life and in spirit. Losing each one of them has been as heartrending as Ming describes, but keeping the conversation going after they drop their ailing bodies has sustained us and changed the grief into awe. In Angels of Rainbow Bridge, Ming Chee has captured the essence of our relationships with our fur babies, and a way to keep the love alive. I am so grateful for Reiki Fur Babies and all their wisdom.

Sara Stein, M.D.
Cleveland, OH
August 28, 2019

*https://www.brainpickings.org/2012/11/07/the-big-new-yorker-book-of-dogs/

**https://reikifurbabies.com/2010/09/08/reiki-for-4-yr-old-newfoundland-injured-by-200lb-brother/

Acknowledgments

I want to express my utmost appreciation to Lori Aldana, editor extraordinaire whom I am so grateful to for helping me publish my inspired works. You help make my life as an author effortless.

I am thankful for Patches, Thumper, Sammy Diva, Mochi, Lucy, and for Jesse who is still with me now in the physical. You are all the inspiration for this book and continue to inspire me in life.

I also would like to thank every fur baby and non-fur creatures for touching me with their souls throughout the years, teaching and guiding me. My heart is so full from learning from all of you.

Preface

I love dogs, but I would have to say it's a fairly new love affair which came about in adulthood. From childhood, it had always been cats for me. Don't get me wrong. I wished for a puppy when I was a kid, but I wasn't allowed to have one. Instead, my parents brought home a kitten. Only to realize that it was most likely because we had mice and they figured the solution would be a cat. But for a kid like me, the bond was instant.

My first cat was a Calico we called Patches. She had a distinctive colored patch over one eye. I also nicknamed her Patchee. (Get it? 'Chee'.) Well, what can I say? She was awesome. My parents thought so, too. Perhaps because the mice were gone within minutes of her arrival, and we were never to be pestered by them again.

Patches was more of an indoor cat, she hardly went outside except for every now and again when I took her out to play. I kept a good eye on her, never letting her out of my sight for fear of losing her.

It's funny how my dad thought she was the smartest cat on the planet because she covered her poop with dirt. I know, 'smartest cat ever.' He didn't even believe me when I told him, "ALL cats do that, dad." So, I let him continue thinking we had the most special cat of all. Of course, to me she was very special anyway.

Sadly, one day my parents made me give her away. Not away to anyone – just away. It made me so sad and guilty at the same time. And for a long time, I think I kept trying to make up for it, even though the adult in me would tell me it wasn't my fault because I was just a child. But the child in me was forever feeling sorry. I would pray for her every single day, and for months I forced my dad to drive me out there to leave her some cat food. Still, it never took the pain away.

That was my first experience with losing a beloved pet. It was a difficult one for me. As I mentioned, I was tormented by guilt alongside the sadness of losing her – well, sort of losing her. The bond was still there though, and I never forgot her to this day.

I realize Patches must have crossed the Rainbow Bridge quite some time ago and it's from there where I imagine she still looks after me. Whether she's still on the other side, or maybe her soul has returned, but what I do feel strongly is that our connection will never be broken no matter where she is.

I'm sorry to say, there really is no preparation for when your fur baby departs. It's never easy. It doesn't get easier. It doesn't feel easier. But, it's a part of life. Acceptance is easier for me because I do not believe in death. Rather, I call this part of life "transitioning." Especially, because I know I can always talk to my fur babies on the other side of the Rainbow Bridge, which is in part what I want to share with you here.

Although, before you continue reading, it's important for me to disclose that I didn't want this book to be too *woo woo*, because my wish is to be able to touch one and all who have lost their pet. My intent is that you and everyone who reads this book can find hope within these pages.

I was inspired when one of my friends told me that because I was so public with my grief, it gave her hope and brought her to the realization that she had never grieved an abortion or the loss of her beloved boxer. In her words, tears were streaming down her cheeks as she saw the outpouring of love that was being shown to me on social media after my beloved Lucy transitioned.

This book was written to help ease a bit of your broken heart after experiencing the loss of your beloved fur baby. And it is broken in half. I get that. I used to scoff at people who would tell me, "Time heals all wounds." Yes, time kind of does, but not really. There are moments of sadness, then there are moments of joy or laughter when happy memories surface.

In my grief, I got spurts of strength to carry on doing what I'm supposed to do while I am still here on this planet – this book is one of them.

I'll be honest, there are times I find myself wishing I was with my fur babies on the other side. Not because I am too sad to carry on, but because of what I discovered they were doing in the afterlife. I take comfort in knowing that one day I will be with them again. If only I could write a book of that experience from over there!

❧1❧

Finding Each Other ~ Mochi, Sammy Diva, Lucy

When I moved to California from Washington, I wanted to adopt a kitten. I found out someone was rehoming a litter of Mainecoons. Mochi was the smallest one in the bunch, though not the prettiest of them all. But, I felt an instant connection with her. Maybe because I, too, was the smallest one in the bunch compared to my siblings. I remember Mochi having these adorable little tufts of hair in her paws, ready for walking on the snow-covered grounds of Maine. Lucky for her, in Los Angeles she wouldn't have to worry about protecting her furry paws from the cold snow.

It was Mochi who taught me that cats surely do have nine lives. Mochi was adventurous. We lived in an apartment with a huge balcony where she loved to walk along the wall. You know, cats can walk across anything. They're like gymnasts. Have you seen those videos of cats doing daredevil stunts, flipping and falling, doing a crazy number of somersaults in the air without touching the floor before finally landing on all fours? That was Mochi. It made me nervous to watch her, but to her it came naturally. When she wasn't up to her stunts, she would bask in the warm sunshine. She loved that balcony.

One day, I came home from work and I couldn't find her. At first, I wasn't worried, but after a few more minutes, it was odd that she wasn't responding to my calls. I combed the entire apartment. She was not inside. That's when I began to freak out. It struck me that a few days before, I had seen some black crows swooping down tormenting the cats around the area who liked to hang. The cats weren't generally afraid of the birds, and perhaps the crows were aware.

In that instant, I instinctively began to fear that something bad had happened to Mochi. I ran down to the main floor from our third-floor apartment and frantically began searching around the perimeters. I don't know how I even found her, because she was balled up in between some bushes around a corner a few meters away from the apartment building. I started to cry as I picked her up ever so gently. She was hurt.

I called my friend and neighbor for help and together we took Mochi to the animal emergency hospital. They immediately took her in to examine her. The vet came out and told me she had to be admitted. *A cat admitted to a hospital?* That was new to me. But she had cracked her palate and there was nothing that could be done except to let it heal on its own. They admitted her for observation and a small IV was placed into her furry paw.

I didn't sleep all night. At midnight, I called to see how Mochi was doing. The nurse informed me that she was being administered pain medication and was calmly resting. Imagining Mochi needing morphine and being hooked up to an IV was bad enough, but I think because I was a pharmacist, the thought of it all was harder to grapple with. I felt so sorry for her in that frail little body. I remember my brother calling me from Washington to console me.

I attributed Mochi's pain and suffering to the crows. It was apparent she had fallen from the balcony where her claw marks were visibly embedded down the side of the wall where she had tried to hang on for dear life. They must have tormented her until they got her to lose her balance, which she NEVER did. The image of the claw marks down the side of the balcony wall and Mochi rolled up in a little ball for hours, waiting for me to find her, broke my heart.

After 24 hours, my angel finally came home. Even though I saved Mochi that time, I must admit, she saved me more. If I would have lost her in that terrible accident, I would not have been able to live with myself. Finding Mochi when she was a kitten and finding Mochi when she was hurt made me realize how deep our connection was. That's why she's my angel to this day.

It was during the Christmas season of 2002 when a very special yellow Labrador came into my life. For a long time, all I wanted was yellow lab. I don't know why, I just did. Finally, one day she popped up on my computer screen during an internet search. I clicked on a weblink to find out more about her. It turned out she was the mother belonging to The Seeing Eye trainers. What a noble profession, I thought. All her babies were service dogs giving back to our society. Now it was time to retire her at just two years old. Perfect timing.

Several miles away, my young niece had written a letter to Santa Claus. She wasn't asking for the latest tech toy or gadget. She asked Santa for her Auntie Ming to receive a dog for Christmas. It seemed that Santa was having a hand in making good on my niece's wish.

Back at home, I had sent a message asking to see the yellow lab's picture. The owners emailed me her picture. When I saw her beautiful face in that photo, it was love at first sight. I knew right then and there we were meant to be together. She was living in the mountains of Northern California, and I was living on the coast of Southern California. The magic of the timing was that my best friend and her husband were driving through there and could pick her up for me.

Her given name was Diva. The owners gave her that name because she had won a beauty contest. When I saw her, I just couldn't change her name, even though Diva was the sort of name, and people who know me would agree, I would never have given to my dog. So, instead I added Sammy, short for Samantha. And now Sammy Diva was home.

Everything seemed new to Sammy Diva – the car, the staircase, even the television. The noises of the city were alarming to her. But day by day, little by little, I taught Sammy Diva how to climb the stairs to the bedroom, to sit and watch TV next to me, cross the streets carefully, and enjoy car rides. Every day we bonded closer and closer together. She was such a love who made my heart sing. I called her my "Sunshine Girl" because of her beautiful yellow coat and face that made me want to sing her *You Are My Sunshine* every time I was around her. I spoiled and loved her every day of her life.

She was also the one who inspired me to be a healer for animals. It was because of Sammy Diva that I learned Reiki and the reason why Reiki Fur Babies exists. Reiki cured her from canine hip dysplasia. She taught me so much over the years. Sammy Diva believed that every dog, cat, and wild animal should have the benefit of health and wellness through energy healing.

Lucy was rescued by my very best friend. Her rescue was dubbed "The Liberation of Lucy." The story begins with my best friend's boxer called Ry who had a very intuitive nature. He was very excited one morning, jumping and looking out the front window. Curious to see what Ry was fussing about, my best friend looked out and saw her neighbor holding a designer leash in her hand, and at the end of that pretty, pink leash was a matching motif collar on the cutest little puppy she'd ever seen. She quickly decided to investigate where this puppy came from. It turned out this little girl was a Pembroke Corgi, all fuzz and smiles, called Lucy Lu.

A couple of days had gone by without seeing Lucy, but Ry on the other hand was frozen to the chair, looking out the window on puppy patrol. Eventually, my best friend noticed that the neighbor and Lucy would walk down the street then back into the house, once a day, all of three minutes spent at best. Her curiosity grew, and finally one day she decided to go over to her neighbor's house to do a bit more sleuthing.

It turns out that Lucy's living situation was very restricted. Lucy lived 22 to 23 hours a day inside of a designer crate in the corner of the dining room. She was only let out for 1 to 2 hours to allow the young twins to play with her. It was a sad situation for my best friend to witness, but even sadder for poor Lucy.

Realizing her neighbor was too busy with her children and life in general, she did what any dog lover would do and offered to sit Lucy and look after her during the day. It was a great arrangement because it also filled Ry up with joy and happiness to have Lucy's company.

But Lucy was still not receiving enough attention when she went back home. Being cooped up in her crate, she would be covered in her own feces. When she was let out of her crate, she would try to run and hide. The family could never hold her because she would bite, cry and shake all the time they tried.

It was very different when she was at my best friend's house. Her husband was very willing to give Lucy warm showers; even my husband would pitch in to help care for Lucy. All of us were naturally falling in love with this little girl, and it was a reciprocal love affair.

There was one weekend me and my best friend were going out of town which meant Lucy would be kept at home, cooped up in her crate. It was awful to imagine, but as soon as we returned Ry greeted us exasperated, running around in circles and sniffing all around. He was looking for Lucy.

My best friend immediately went over to the neighbor's house to pick her up. When she got there she was told Lucy had run away. Not just once, but *seven* times. On top of that, she was at one point kidnapped by some boys, except a couple noticed that Lucy was trying to escape from them, so they approached the boys and they let her go. Thank god Lucy had a collar with a phone number. It was clear that Lucy was looking for her secondary home.

My best friend convinced the family to let her find Lucy a good home. They admitted that they lived very busy lives and did not have the time and energy to give Lucy the care and attention she required. So, they agreed. Lucy went to live with my best friend. But she also spent a lot of time at my house and sometimes weekend sleep overs with Sammy Diva and Mochi. Lucy became a part of our extended family.

One thing my best friend and I both noticed was this amazing thing that Lucy did. She had two routines in two different homes which included her eating habits, her walking habits, even sleeping habits. The moment she walked into our house, she knew what routine she would be in. At my best friend's house, she lived another. We thought, what a smart dog because we had never seen anything like it. Lucy was comfortable at both our houses.

I was pretty happy with our little fur family, Sammy Diva and Mochi, but Lucy wormed her way into my heart. I didn't know I had room in my heart for one more dog, but I was becoming very attached to Lucy. It became harder for me to just pick up Sammy Diva after work and leave Lucy behind.

My best friend developed a lung problem and could no longer let Lucy sleep on her bed which she was accustomed to at both our houses. After a lot of consideration for what was in Lucy's best interest, we got together and decided that Lucy should live with me. We commemorated the event with a puppy shower to celebrate her adoption which included guests, presents, and a fabulous caterer.

That is the story of Lucy's liberation. Ry was the rescuer, and my best friend was the facilitator. And the Corgi, well, she was never a dog-dog. She was a dog-person. There is no other more special, amazing, intelligent, sweetest dog other than Lucy. The Pembroke Corgi who from a baby had two homes, two families, without being confused or unhappy. Lucy was one happy fur baby who knew she equally had the love of all of us.

❧ 2 ❧

Saying Goodbye ~ Facing Transition Is Never Easy

It should have been a usual routine morning for me that day, but something was about to change, forever. Lucy did something completely different and out of character. She came up to me while I was still sleeping and BARKED. I woke up and noticed Mochi wasn't on the bed with Lucy – dog and cat always slept together, it was the sweetest thing to watch.

That morning, I knew Lucy was alerting me to Mochi. Was she under my bed, I wondered? I crawled under the king-sized bed and sure enough, I found Mochi there. I literally had to crawl under the bed to get close enough to her to hear and see what was going on. She was making a sound that clearly did not sound good – a scary noise, like she was gasping for air.

I started bawling as I dragged her fragile body out and I could feel her resisting. I wrapped her in a towel. My first reaction was to Reiki her, then I realized…my little girl was dying. *How could this be happening? She hadn't even shown signs of sickness!*

Mochi was clearly in pain, but I was afraid to take her to the vet because I didn't want her to be traumatized. I wanted her to leave this earth peacefully. I ran to get her some water and called my best friend who was also my Reiki partner. When she arrived, she told me I needed to take Mochi to the vet. In shock, I managed to find the cat carrier and with my best friend's help, we carefully placed Mochi in it and drove her to the vet's office.

The entire time on the way there, I was talking to Mochi, crying, telling her how much I loved her, thanking her for being part of my life. I even found myself telling her it was okay for her to go. When we arrived at the vet's office, they took Mochi into triage immediately. The vet came out a few moments later and said she could barely hear Mochi's heart because there was probably a mass over it. Her organs were shutting down. She must've had tumor that burst.

Then came the dreaded question. I already knew the answer. I would tell all my clients to do right by their fur baby whenever they asked for advice in situations like this one, and here I was facing the same heart wrenching moment. In tears, I nodded a yes. It was my turn to return the favor and let Mochi go.

The vet stepped out of the room to arrange for the medication. My best friend and I began to Reiki Mochi again. She was no longer panting or even crying, she was incredibly still. My best friend took her into her arms and held her against her heart. She told me Mochi was expressing so much gratitude to me for doing this for her. And at that very moment, Mochi turned to look at me. I sobbed and cried while massaging her little ears in my hands – they felt so cold.

I was so grateful that I had the chance to say everything I wanted to say to Mochi. All I wanted was for her not to be in pain anymore. Then the vet walked in to administer the medication. It was incredible as I witnessed Mochi leaving her body, the 7-pound shell of Mainecoon fur that had housed her soul. She was so light in spirit. And just like that, she was gone, peacefully.

The grief came in waves, sadness and tears came and went. I missed her terribly. I missed seeing her bowl. I missed her loud mouth. I asked her to come visit me in my dreams.

She's my angel and for 15 years she heard all my secrets, seen the places I've lived, and known the people and fur babies I've loved. She had taught me so much in life, and she would teach me even more in her passing.

Mochi, I will never forget you. I love you.

Little did I know when I woke up the morning of December 16, how that day would mark an upsetting weekend ahead because my sweet yellow lab and best fur-friend for 11 years would be making her transition. Thinking back, I must honestly say that I mourned her transition from the day I got her. The bond between us was so strong, I could *not* imagine not having her.

Year after year, if the thought of her transitioning crossed my mind, I would literally cry. It was my best friend who told me I must have grieved Sammy Diva's loss the entire time she was with me. I could not help it. Then that day actually came.

I was sitting at my computer when I suddenly heard a cry. It was coming from Sammy Diva. She was in the hallway where she liked to lay, and I could sort of hear she was struggling to get up. It was only after a couple of attempts, that I heard her cry out. I think she had forgotten I was home.

As soon as I heard the cry, I quickly got up and rushed to her. She was slipping with every step because she couldn't get enough traction. It completely broke my heart. Watching her age over the last few years was so difficult, but to see her physically suffering was more than I could bear to watch.

I held her and reassured her she was okay, that I was there with her. I searched around looking for a way she could walk across the tiled floor. I made a dash around the house collecting all the rugs and floor carpets and used them to line the hallway in hopes it would make it easier for her to walk on.

I dreaded having to face making the painful decision. Here was Sammy Diva, so faithful and loyal and loving. We had been through so much together, and it was she who inspired me to BE exactly where I was. But in that moment, it was not about me.

I recalled how my best friend's Boxer had requested not to suffer by undergoing chemo after only five years in his physical body. Quality of life is as important to a fur baby as it is to a human being. Sammy Diva had so much dignity. Even though she let me wipe her bottom, she was still one proud girl.

The day before Sammy Diva crossed over, I had the sense from her that she was needed to do something *bigger* on the other side. What? I don't know. But what I did know then was, the time had come for to depart because she was having trouble breathing. Her breathing became shallow and it scared her. I knew what I needed to do.

That night, I laid down next to Sammy Diva and promised her that I would not let her suffer. I was not going to keep her alive just for my selfish, albeit love-driven benefit, if I thought she was suffering needlessly for one second. I loved her too much for that. She listened and gave me a kiss.

Fortunately, a couple of years earlier, I had decided to set aside a fund so that when the time came if Sammy Diva needed assistance to transition, I wouldn't be strapped for money. Mind you, this was a time when I was going through deep contrast which I detail in my book *Money Blues to Blue Money*.

Just before the vet assistance arrived, I can recall having a feeling of nervousness – it wasn't just me, but I could sense Sammy Diva, too. Or perhaps it was me projecting onto Sammy Diva.

I remember taking her outside where I gave her a big

cuddle under the bright shining sun and feeling the warmth of our love. She managed to pee before she sauntered back inside where my brother, sister-in-law and best friend were gathered along with Lucy and Charlie, my brother's chihuahua, to be with her.

The assisting vet was a godsend, and together we all created a sacred space in my living room. We had a little ceremony where we said a prayer and called in the angels. I could sense Ry's presence was there, Sammy Diva's best friend in this life. He was waiting for her soul to soar.

As I held her and soothed her, she quietly and peacefully slipped away. I will never forget the moment that her bigger than life spirit soared and left her beautiful fur body on the dog bed in my living room.

I know that our souls will forever be connected. Sammy Diva is a treasure that I will always have so much gratitude for. We'll continue this journey together wherever our souls exist.

I love you Sammy Diva.

༄

As my Corgi, Lucy, was aging, she needed a little more attention from me. It was so difficult to see her age – just downright painful. The first thing I noticed was she started to lose her hearing. I had to tap her on the shoulder to get her attention. Then her back legs started giving out and she would literally fall. I would help carry her down the stairs because she was able to go up, but not down. She also needed to go outside a little more often. *Sigh.* But she still had her heart-melting smile, her spunk.

So, when the time came, I'd like to say I knew, but not from the start. Lucy had been on CBD oil and had been responding well to it. The first thing I noticed when she was started on CBD oil was how much better her legs were feeling. She looked happier. I do believe it relieved her symptoms. And, looking back, I'm glad that I was able to give her something to make her days leading up to her transition more comfortable.

On that day, the decision came fast. Lucy made it very clear to me it was time for her to go. There were so many tears and so much pain. As I am writing this, Lucy has only been gone exactly one month today. Although I am in a better place with grief, the story of her final day is still too fresh to tell in detail. Instead, I'd rather give a eulogy, a tribute to her:

I love this Corgi. I have known her for over 14 years. She was such a spit fire. She has taught me so many things. She taught me to ask for what I want. She showed me it was okay to stand up for myself. She showed me how to be flexible.

Lucy was adored by so many. She knew that. She loved that. Cars would literally stop in the middle of traffic just to get a look at her. I remember, once this car full of tourists stopped in Venice Beach to take pictures of her. She loved that. She had the greatest smile. She loved children. She loved people. She was the extrovert that I am not. She was a Rockstar. She made me laugh with her swearing and taught me it is okay to say the F-word.

I loved all her nicknames: Lucy Lu, Beanster, Lulu Bean, Loose Goose…and sometimes I just called her Corgi. Because she is an amazing Corgi. She lived and walked as if she were the size of a German Shepherd.

Knowing that I was going to be saying good-bye to her soon, was not what I was quite expecting that day, that is until she let me know. What kept me sane was knowing her soul is forever connected to mine – knowing I will be seeing her in my dreams.

I miss her physical presence so much. She was a spitfire! And she was a spitfire till the day she soared away.

Lucy, I love you.

വു

Signs that your fur baby is nearing her time to transition may not be noticeable in advance, and in many cases, not revealed to you until that same day. Her behavior will be off, or her health will take a sudden turn. With cats, as was my experience and going by what I've heard, they usually go hide somewhere if they are ill or soon to be crossing over. In Mochi's case, it was Lucy who found her. It felt like I only had a few minutes to say good bye to her, though lucky enough to have had the chance to.

The hardest but most kind thing to do is to not let your fur baby suffer. I made a promise to myself and to my fur babies that they would not suffer pain or discomfort in their last moments. Personally, I chose to trade their suffering for my own after they transitioned. Meaning, enduring the pain of releasing them and suffering their loss over waiting for their illness to take its course to keep them with me longer.

On the other hand, some people feel it unbearable to let go of their animals and so unfortunately their fur baby may suffer a little longer for their human. It is very difficult to let go. I understand. And I do not judge anyone who struggles with making the decision. But, if you can, look deep into your heart, and if you trust me and believe that your fur baby is going to a better place – then you may find it easier to let him go.

If possible, make the decision early on to make a pact with your fur baby that when the time nears, you will save him from suffering. I know I wish the same for me when my time comes, and you probably would want the same, too – no suffering at the end of life.

A friend of mine had a dog who towards the end would howl and scream from the bone pain he was in. I heard it several times, and it was chilling and very sad. Until one of our friends finally said out of love, "It's okay to let him go."

It's understandable to not want to be the one who makes the decision of 'when it's time.' Sometimes you just need permission from someone else that it is okay to make that decision. Just know that when you let your fur baby go, you are letting him go out of love. You will soon discover that that love will come pouring back to you (after the grief process).

This is just a practical suggestion, but if you can, save some money aside when you know your fur baby has an illness, it will make it easier to call on an in-house vet or to take them to the vet to get euthanized. I have done it both ways. I took Mochi to the vet and they were very kind and compassionate. With Sammy Diva, I had the blessing of having a vet come to the house.

The easiest, of course, would be if they transitioned on their own, in their sleep, feeling no pain. I wish it were that simple, a peaceful transition. In fact, I have told my fur babies to please go like this when it's their time. But, that has never been the experience for me. Nope, they have always asked for my assistance.

So, how do you say good bye to your beloved fur baby? Writing down your feelings for her is one way to get all your emotions out. I wrote tributes to my fur babies. Although, with Lucy, I wrote about her before she left so it wasn't past tense. Yes, I've said goodbye to them in flooding tears, but I managed to do it. And in that space, they also said their goodbyes to me.

One other thing I'd suggest, while your fur baby is alive – snap pictures. Take zillions of them. Record video. Save them on your smartphone, tablet, laptop or on social media. I was never so happy to see social media memories of my Lucy pop up right after she joined the troops of Rainbow Bridge. It was as though she was letting me know she would always be with me.

One of the most important things I have realized with the passing of all the animals is that when their soul leaves the body, it is clear to see that the body is really just a shell. Their soul lives on.

❦ 3 ❧

Healing from Sorrow ~ Overcoming Grief with Love

Who created this thing called "grief" anyways, right? It would be so much easier to skip that part of life. Unfortunately, life doesn't work that way though. And while grief is certainly not a fun ride, it is a necessary one. There is only one way to get off that ride which is to find a way to cope and move forward. Possibly the most compassionate thing you can do for yourself is to let your grief be – give yourself permission to grieve.

This reminds me of something remarkable I watched Lucy do when Sammy Diva transitioned. Lucy told Sammy to not let herself be seen for two weeks so that she could grieve. I thought, *how smart was this Corgi to allow herself space to grieve?* She would build herself huts with blankets each night on the couch and then burrow herself inside them. In my life, I had never seen anything like it.

Anyone who knows me for a second knows my mantra:

What you focus on grows.

So, after I released Lucy and allowed myself to grieve her, mourn her…I turned my focus on love. I focused on all the love I felt for Lucy. Yes, my heart still ached, but what I got in response was completely amazing. I felt Lucy's love in return. It came in the form of an outpouring of love all around me. Friends, family, acquaintances and even people I've never met – all over social media – were expressing their support and love. I got letters, messages, notes, phone calls, texts, flowers and plants, cards and gift baskets. The love kept pouring in for days.

After a few days went by with the passing of Lucy, I had good days and okay days. The nights were especially difficult for me, more so than mornings. At times, though, it switched, and I'd find myself waking up some mornings wanting to stay in bed and not wanting to get up for yoga. The first time it happened, I forced myself to go even though I wanted to curl up with sadness.

Let me be clear. By forcing myself to get out of bed and go to my yoga class, this wasn't me not giving myself space to grieve. Rather, it was me focusing on self-love. Love is the highest vibration we can achieve. When we raise our vibration to love we are taken care of – like being transported to a place where we are surrounded by love. So, by raising my vibration with self-love, I came to a space where I was totally supported by love.

The sorrow you feel with losing your fur baby, or any loved one for that matter, is immense and you probably will feel like you can't go on or you can't make it through the grief. But try to that remember it's all about how you feel that matters. Try not to think what your fur baby must be feeling because she is in 'heaven.' So, when you feel as though your whole world is crumbling inside you, try focusing on feeling self-love. You might just be surprised with the discovery of what you are surrounded by.

I can say with certainty that LOVE always triumphs. As a confirmation, Lucy came to me during yoga class. When I opened my eyes, I could still see her. I was so full of gratitude to feel the connection with her in that moment. I thanked her and asked her to keep giving me her guidance.

When you're grieving, healing may seem impossible and practicing self-love is probably the last thing on your mind. All you want to do is hold on to the memories of your beloved fur baby. But imagine shifting your pain towards love. What would it feel like to raise your vibration to receiving all that resides in that higher vibration: love, joy, peace, healing? Immerse yourself in that feeling.

As I tuned into the love I felt for my fur baby, not the pain of losing her, I felt love from her back. I knew she was with me and showering me with her love. It was reflected in all the outpouring of love I mentioned before.

If you find it difficult to raise your vibration during the grieving process, remember this: even a little shift, a slight thought, a bit of focus on love, will bring you healing. Notice when you are feeling sadness and pain and use affirmations of love:

I am filled with love.
I will always be supported by love.
The love from my loved one is everywhere I am.

Notice the things you love around you. No matter what it is, whether it's something tangible or an awareness of something. You may be able to find it by looking within your home, your friends, your career. Then when you find that something, tap into its abundant energy and feel the deliciousness of it.

Try shifting the physical around you. Sometimes just making a little outward change or bringing something new into your life can shift the inside feelings. One day when I was hurting from the thought of me not having Sammy Diva's physical presence around me, she came to me and told me to make peace with that thought. Then she told me to take her stuffed rabbit to be the physical presence I missed. While thinking of her, I held the toy and hugged it against my heart. Sure enough, she was right. It did fill a void.

Animal communication is real, you just need to be open to it. Hiring an animal communicator can be very healing. Even though I am one, I still sought an animal communicator when Sammy Diva and Lucy transitioned. Reason being, the grief I felt was too much to bear and I couldn't establish the right connection with them immediately afterward. And it was really comforting to know that on the other side my fur babies were happy and thriving. Sammy Diva said she felt lighter – and Lucy, she was flying!

Lucy made sure to let me know that I had made the right choices. This was important for me to hear as I grieved. During such an emotional time, your mind can play tricks on you, making you question if you really did do the right thing or should you have done something different. But

Lucy opened some doors for me, confirming the messages I received through animal communication. She even confirmed that writing this book would heal not just me, but many, many others going through the grief of missing their best friend.

☙ 4 ❧

Soul Journey ~ Discovering A Deeper Connection

A few nights after Lucy transitioned, I had a visit from Sammy Diva and Mochi in a dream. They told me *"The trifecta is together."* I found myself feeling somewhat jealous of how happy Lucy was on the other side now that she had joined Sammy Diva and Mochi – the three of them all together. I missed her. I wanted to feel that joy with them.

In the grand scheme of things, though, I was grateful for this awareness. And it brought me so much joy knowing that my departed fur babies were united, guiding me. They all were still working on my behalf.

No, it's not farfetched to hear, see or feel the presence of your fur baby when he is not physically with you. Just as it's possible to have a deep connection with your fur baby when he is alive, it's also possible to continue having that connection once he's crossed over the Rainbow Bridge. Because you or your fur baby might not realize the power he has until he gets to the other side. But if you stay open to it, he'll show you.

Looking back, I know that when Patches was left in the park that day it marked a turning point for me in my journey. My soul was either to choose a path to love and help animals or turn my heart away for it had been so broken.

I am a Reiki Master who assists animals – it's clear the journey I chose for this life time. Not everyone, however, needs to be a Reiki Master or an animal communicator to establish a connection with their fur baby. All it really is, is a bond. A bond beyond space and time that can never be broken.

When we held Sammy Diva's ceremony on the day of her transition, one of the attendees gave a beautiful invocation bringing in the angels and archangels for Sammy's crossing over. We talked with Sammy sharing and recalling fun times and stories with her best friend Ry, who of course came in spirit to accompany her, along with faeries and spirit animals.

The house was filled with the presence of light energy. Imagine a line of divine beings, spirit animals and departed souls present from royalty faeries to mice and donkeys that Reiki Fur Babies had sent healing to – all there to greet Sammy Diva as they hailed, "The Great One is back!" For me, it was this sense along the lines of the Lion Aslan from *The Chronicles of Narnia* returning home. It was truly a wonderment to witness such a grand connection.

Three months after Sammy Diva transitioned, she was

still by my side in spirit. In her afterlife, she continued to teach me – about loss and how it really isn't a loss. The word transition meant something so much more to me. It represented movement, passage, or change from one position, state, stage, concept to another. Once I realized this, I removed the word "die" from my vocabulary. Sammy Diva, Lucy, Mochi haven't died in my belief. I'm able to connect with them whenever I want. All I need to do is close my eyes and ask them to come, and they appear.

I had a very special experience with the transformation of Sammy Diva. Notice that I'm using the word "transformation" and not "transition" to describe this experience. This is because the day before Sammy Diva left her physical body, she herself called it that. This is how I knew she was needed on the other side.

She said, *"More will be revealed after the transformation has happened. There is much work to be done form the non-physical, and even though I am sad to be leaving this plane, this body is so hard to be in and I look forward to feeling good again. I will be able to help you so much more than I can now, and the work we will do together, all of us, will be brought into a level of greatness that has never been seen before."*

When I asked Sammy Diva if she would be coming back to the physical, she said she wasn't sure because the things she needed to do, needed to be done from the non-physical world. She went on to say that once the shift of what we were doing occurs, *"I'll see if coming back is something that will happen."*

As her spirit soared and left her beautiful body, I never imagined what I would experience and write about later was something that could exist in this reality. The journey, a very deeply connected one in the spiritual world, was in the works. And it didn't just happen to me, it happened to many people I love and care about. Sammy Diva continued to reveal herself to me and in the lives of those I had a strong connection or bond with.

During my Reiki sessions she would show up not only as her physical image, but she would light up like a fireball. I could see her body and I could feel the heat of her powerfulness. This was the beginning of her work. I learned that her healing power would be sent through my Reiki like an electronic charge.

All I, or anyone who wanted her healing had to do was set the intention and she would fortify and strengthen the intention, going after the disease or illness that was in the body. She would appear to us in visions, dreams, signs, communication, and even 5D and 7D consciousness. It was through these streams of awareness that she introduced and gave us *honeycomb* healing. More on that later.

I asked Sammy Diva to come to me one day and she appeared eating honeycomb. This is what I called it because of how it looked to me and I also "heard" the word itself. The shape resembled the honeycomb from bees. As I watched her eat it, I asked if I could have some. Sammy Diva started giving me this honeycomb on a daily basis.

As time went on, I began to realize this box of light, meaning the honeycomb, was healing. It was a sustenance for her as well as healing for me, but I would discover it was not solely meant for me. It was for all beings to have.

I started hearing from multiple people that Sammy Diva had come to them and healed or helped with big shifts in their lives. Some called on Sammy Diva for help, and with others she just appeared on her own. She was giving them the honeycomb, too. And every time I would hear their testimony, it was accompanied by how much Sammy Diva loved me. Not only was this comforting, but it brought so much joy in the aftermath of my grief.

I felt so plugged-in to Sammy Diva that my grief began to subside. Yes, from time to time I would still tear up at the memory of her, but I could feel her so intently during that time. I can remember feeling like she wasn't really "gone."

For Sammy Diva to continue her soul journey by my side was such a blessing. She helped me through some of the most difficult times of my life being on the other side. Sammy Diva really gave back to me what I gave to her in this life time, and so much more.

It is mind blowing to know that my once physical dogs and cats are now beautiful beings of Rainbow Bridge, but even more amazing is knowing that they are star children from the same star I am.

ॐ 5 ॐ

Spirit Lives On ~ Signs, Visits & Messages from Rainbow Bridge

In my experience as a Reiki master, I have found that animals have a way to get messages to us by amazing means. Like the recent visit from my pet rabbit who was called Thumper. It felt like he basically *thumped* at me, *"Hey, what am I – chopped liver?"* I smiled and chuckled as he came in loud and clear. After Lucy transitioned, I was flooded with memories of my other fur babies, but I don't know why it had been awhile since I had thought of Thumper. Good for him for not letting me forget!

So, the story of Thumper, as I remember from my childhood, was that I chose him from a sea of white bunnies because he was the only grey one. His name may have been inspired by the bunny character in *Bambi*, but he really did thump with one of his hind legs.

The best way I knew how to take care of him when I was a child was to keep Thumper safe in his cage, letting him out now and then to play. Cliché as it may sound, had I known what I know now, I would have done more for him. But all I remember is we had a lot of fun together.

I have a vivid memory of him bolting down the stairs and hopping all around the house like a wild bunny as I chased after him. Sadly, too, this was the day he transitioned. In my child's mind, I pictured make-believe stories of how and why he had to leave. I suppose I did this to help me cope with my loss.

Curiously, when I was going through some painful and trying times in my adult life that I talk about in my book *Money Blues to Blue Money*, Thumper paid me several visits. I did a lot of astral traveling then which is different from dreaming.

I have always been a big dreamer, so I could tell the difference when I'm dreaming, when I'm in a different dimension or even when I'm living a parallel life. When I'm astral traveling, I can actually taste the cake I'm eating or touch the fabric of a sheet. I can even smell Sammy Diva's distinct smell that she has, and I can feel the softness of her fur.

Thumper showed up in my astral travels as a warrior rabbit – wearing warrior gear and standing tall as we engaged in battle together against dark forces. Knowing that he is and always will be around for me brings me so much comfort. More importantly, however, I learned that our fur babies on the other side are quite powerful. They have extreme powers and abilities as expanded beings to help us heal and even manifest.

This also reminds me of Mochi coming back to me in astral traveling. She was also part of my team, so to speak, during times of contrast. Mochi had the gift of creating 'grids' as in, if you think of an electronic or laser grid around your home for protection – that was her specialty. She even did it for friends. She came through for one friend who asked her for a portable grid that she could have around her at work to protect her from negative energy.

It's interesting that Corgis are the faeries' favorite for riding in battle. It was during one of my astral travels that Lucy showed up in warrior mode, too. Through the dim lighting, I managed to see her bright red and white fur draped in battle gear. All my senses knew it was her. Although I was so happy to see her, I could also sense that she was not visiting me for play – we had work to do.

One day I suggested to a friend that she ask Lucy for help on a project. I was half kidding unsure if this friend would be able to hear Lucy. But, I was only half surprised when she came back and said that, sure enough, Lucy had come to her fast and strong with all kinds of ideas. *Wow!* That's when I realized that Lucy, like my other fur babies, was doing wonderful work on the other side. She was after all attuned to Reiki in the physical, so it's no wonder she had resumed her work in spirit form. When I heard how she was showing up for others who are my friends, my grief shifted to manageable.

This is what transition is all about – changing form yet remaining connected. As I think back, when Sammy Diva first transitioned, I remember friends telling me they also had visits from her. So, when my intuitive friends told me they were receiving visits from my transitioned fur babies it warmed my heart and profoundly helped lessen my grief.

One friend told me she was hiking through the mountains when she connected to Sammy Diva in meditation. Another friend told me Sammy Diva showed up every time she had a doctor's appointment which was a very stressful time for her. She would never fail to show up in the front seat of her car as she drove herself to the doctor's office. I can't make this stuff up – this is what people told me!

One day at work, I was in my cubicle doing pharmacy consults. Out of the blue my youngest brother sent me a text. He said he was doing mediation with Charlie his chihuahua. The connection here is that Charlie, who was rescued by my best friend and Reiki Fur Baby partner, became my brother's forever dog.

During the meditation, my brother said that a cat named Patches came through. What was intriguing is that my brother was too young to have any memory of Patches and I'm not sure he really knows what happened that day in the park. Yet, he said she told him to tell me that she was okay and to forgive myself – she was not upset with me. Here I was, decades later, but the healing that occurred on that day did give me great peace knowing that Patches was a healer on the other side and obviously doing some amazing things.

I believe that animals can come back as other animals or as someone else. My joke with Lucy is that she comes back as my bestie with red hair and not necessarily as a dog. Sammy Diva said her best life was with me and would not come back as a yellow lab again. When I heard this, part of me was sad but part of me also understood she had a bigger job to do and is assisting many beings on our planet.

Like humans, while animals are here on the planet in 3D they may not remember what their soul remembers – that they are spiritual beings on the other side of the veil. However, there are animals currently in this dimension that do know this. Just as we human beings can grow spiritually, so can animals. For example, it was a horse who told me that Reiki came from a star. Without going into too much detail, that message resonated with me based on my own spiritual experiences with healing.

Spiritual growth is a personal journey. Sammy Diva taught me that she is not omnipresent like the angels, however, she can be in more than one place. She can wear like 10 different hats. I think she probably knows a lot more now, but this is what I remember finding out shortly after she transitioned. Her transition taught me more than I could ever have imagined.

One of many messages Sammy Diva sent me via an animal communicator was, *"I will always love you, this was the best life of many lives. We have a lot to do, this is not a vacation. We have work to do and [your work] is going to take off even more. Strap on your big girl shoes, make sure you are ready for it."*

She also gave me a glimpse into the being she had transformed into from the physical form. She described it as having been in a size 30 body which felt like stuff was holding her back and now she was a size 6 feeling light, at peace and with more energy. She said, *"Oh, this is what energy feels like."*

It was not at all like when she was sitting around and laying in her physical body, now she felt she could do a whole lot more. She asked that when I did my Reiki sessions to connect with her and I would be able to feel her even more connected that ever. Her healing would be invoked through Reiki like an electronic charge or fireball. This was her way of doing a lot more work than she ever did in physical form. Whenever I would set the intention for healing, Sammy's healing would also come forth to fortify and strengthen that intention. Now I understood why I saw her appear and light up like a fireball during my Reiki sessions.

I loved receiving Sammy Diva's messages as I moved through my grief. I heeded her request to put on my 'big girl shoes' and went to work with my heart love, Sammy. Every new day was an incredible blessing on this journey with her. I couldn't wait to see what would come forth next.

And that's just how it is when you open your heart to receive the power and wonderment of your fur baby after transition. There is so much more to live and experience with your fur baby if you choose to go on that journey.

A couple of days after Lucy transitioned, I was still in excruciating pain from missing her, and as I was taking a shower I could see her silhouette on the tiled wall. I kept blinking my eyes, but every time I opened them, I could still see it. Then to my right on the shower door the letter B came to form. I looked at it and wondered, *B*? Then, I heard *"Just Be."*

From that point forward, even to this day, if I ask for

Lucy, I soon come across the letter **B** on a license plate as I'm driving, on a sign as I walk by, or just anywhere out of nowhere. This is my way of knowing that Lucy is teaching me to "just be."

Your fur baby may be sending you signs, if you pay attention. You may think they're coincidences, but you should trust your inner guidance and, also, trust that your fur baby is sending you a sign.

I went to Southern California for a long weekend. This trip had been planned prior to Lucy's transition. My best friend and I got stuck in Malibu with no wi-fi for several hours at a restaurant. As we were trying to get an Uber, what did I see, but a baby Corgi. Of course, I ran over to her. Of course, it was a sign from Lucy. My friend even made the observation, exclaiming, "I have never even seen a baby Corgi!!"

I was at a dealership a week later getting my car checked out. I had to leave the car overnight. As one of my friends was calling me on my phone to tell me she was there to pick me up, in walked two Corgis! What were the chances of that? I bent down in glee and pet them as they came in as I told the owner proudly, "I have one too!"

I have always asked my fur babies to visit me in dreams. For me, dreams are the perfect gateway for connecting. In this dream, I remember going on a bike ride with Mochi. It was such a magical dream. The next morning, she literally dropped cat litter next to the bed to make sure my brain processed that I was dreaming and connecting to her and not my two dogs. I laughed when I realized the connection. There was no logical way for the cat litter to show up there.

Take it from me, you will find that your fur baby still retains her sense of humor and personality when connecting with you.

Another way you can connect with your transitioned pet is to look for signs that your fur baby would send you from the other side – such as the sound of a wind chime, a song that suddenly plays on the radio, or like how Lucy did, running into your fur baby's breed when you least expect it. I used to sing to Sammy Diva *You Are My Sunshine*, a song not commonly heard, but every time I would hear it, I'd be brought to tears of sentimental joy to know that she was around me.

I was fascinated to discover that Lucy could send me a sign through color. I know what you're thinking, dogs cannot see color. But Lucy's favorite color was pink, I know for sure. I was in a department store one day and I passed by the jewelry counter. I was led intuitively to look down and I saw a brilliant pink heart. I instantly knew it was Lucy. Yes, of course I bought the necklace!

Two months after Lucy transitioned, I was opening the sliding door to let in Jesse the cockapoo. It was nightfall, so it was dark outside. As I was waiting for Jesse, who is black in color, I saw a black blur come into the house and go up the stairs! It startled me so much that I had to do a double take to make sure it wasn't Jesse who had come in running. Then, I realized that Jesse was in fact still outside!

Coincidentally, my best friend happened to be standing there and I said to her, "Did you see that?" She did. We both thought it might be Lucy.

It was such a surprise because I had never seen anything like that with my own eyes. In meditation, yes. In dreams, yes. But not eyes wide open and certainly not so unexpectedly. I wasn't sure whether to sage or not. Anyway, I went to sleep, and everything was fine. I didn't sense anything scary, but I have to say it took me aback.

Then a week later, this time it was daylight, again I opened the sliding door and in came that same black blur and up the stairs it went. I called out, "Lucy, that is you, right?" I decided to get a second opinion and one of our own Reiki Fur Babies' Reiki Masters tuned in and connected with Lucy. She reported back:

"Morning! I connected and wow. Always a wow with you. The blur is Lucy. She said she was glad the grief is lifting, and you can see her at home. Home is the hardest. The blur appears black to you but it's actually ALL the colors. Rainbow light. Lucy said you will see it in meditation when you're ready. Human eyes can only see a small part of this light."

It makes sense, because in life, Lucy was always funny and made me laugh. Sammy Diva would never do anything like that. So, my advice to you, keep open to the personality of your fur babies after they transcend because it might seem like something strange is going on when in fact it's just your fur baby paying you a little visit.

You can contact a trusted animal communicator as an effective means to connect with your transitioned fur baby like I did. However, if for whatever reason you don't want to hire an animal communicator, simply try asking your fur baby, in fact maybe even before she transitions, that you would like her to send you a sign to let you know she's okay.

But what if your fur baby transitioned on his own, or if his passing was an accident and you couldn't ask him before he left? It's okay. Your fur baby can still hear you even though you cannot see him in the physical. Just set the intention and call on him. More often than not, he will respond to you in his own special way that only you will recognize.

✿6✾

The Chronicles of Sammy Diva ~ Life Doesn't End

I've learned from each experience that after a fur baby transitions from her physical body, her being goes through ascension akin to human beings. Just imagine, the body a fur baby inhabited is left by the soul and ascends to another dimension where it takes on other forms. I get that this might be hard to imagine, but I ask that you be open-minded to this possibility. When I did this, it led me on an awe-inspiring journey of afterlife discovery.

Even though Sammy Diva had taken another form after she transitioned, she would still visit me as a yellow lab. To me, it was especially sweet and touching for her to appear this way because she knew I lovingly identified with her in canine form. It was during these special visits she told me I would be experiencing seventh dimension. And, it happened during a guided meditation when my crown chakra was opened which allowed me to understand so much more about the body, the soul and the afterlife.

I have Sammy Diva to thank for this miraculous journey and I believe she is guiding me to share with you this personal experience that showed me what was happening on the other side of Rainbow Bridge.

When I began writing *The Chronicles of Sammy Diva*, I certainly didn't think they would become regular blog posts, let alone part of this book. At first, I thought it would be not only healing, but also fun to talk to her. Then she became sort of a 'soul guide' for me (she was after all the mother of pups from The Seeing Eye). It began shortly after Sammy Diva transitioned when I got a message from a fellow Reiki Master. It gave me goosebumps from head to toe:

"Ming! Sammy just let me know what she's doing! She is BUILDING your Mystery School University on The Other Side! She has a lot of input in how it's going to be. Apparently, she has done this kind of thing in the past and needs ger total focus to make sure it is 'done right' and meets HER standards!!! She wants you to know."

With the transition of Sammy Diva, I began to experience new things. Each week was full of something new, different, and for lack of a better word, magical. The first thing I noticed was that I could see her and everything she was doing while I was awake. I was not dreaming, not meditating – I would simply be thinking about her and she would appear.

Next thing, I would find myself viewing what she was doing at that time. Think of it as turning on the TV and you tune into a movie already showing. I wasn't sure whether it was the beginning, middle or end, but it was a window into her world.

I missed Sammy's physical presence so much, although this deeper knowing of her soul connecting with my intuition would let me know when I could see her. She allowed me to watch and I did not ask questions. I was seeing different planes where time is not separated. It made me so joyful to hear her say she thanked me for allowing her to do her work while I was still grieving.

The first week she was off here and there sending healing to people in my 'world.' The second week she was doing a lot of mind-blowing healing on a galactic level and showing up in my Reiki healing and attunement practices. I partnered with fellow lightworkers, who were also being visited by Sammy Diva, to attune the animal beings of our planet. She began assisting us with the attunements of wild animals we were doing.

In the beginning, she was part of the attunement of the wolves, coyotes, hyenas and jackals. Across oceans and lands Sammy Diva was spreading Reiki to each one of them. She was also seen running alongside the wild dogs and attuning them all. We moved on attuning the feral cats and big cats like lions and tigers asking Sammy Diva to join in with her galactic healing.

Whenever I conducted Reiki attunements, Sammy Diva would be involved adding in her magical part after I was done. She recognized how important doing these attunements in this physical time here on this planet were. I experienced so many shifts along the way.

She was so proud of the work she could do now that she had transitioned, especially proud to be helping "mom" (me) and making me proud. It was a fantastic experience.

By the third week she had completed something big. I tuned into her and I saw a happy DANCING dog! That's when I knew she would be sharing with me what she was doing on the other side, the significance of her healing work, and how she was including me in the unfolding.

I loved that she was sharing all of this with me and how elated her soul was. She said she was able to do so much more now that she was back in her soul body. She had the ability to be in several places at the same time, at different times.

Sammy showed me she had her paws in a lot of pies, doing a lot of things, shifting and changing. It was like she was in a kitchen with many different mixing bowls, all at the same time, and able to handle them with confidence.

One morning when I connected to Sammy Diva, I saw her sitting ON a galaxy of stars. It made me smile, filling my heart with happiness. I felt so blessed being able to share that magical moment with her. She could walk the stars. I would later see her walk ON the stars. I knew it was the beginning of a whole new journey, and this was part of it.

About three months later, Sammy Diva had not left my side for the most part. She had been teaching me so much about loss and how it really wasn't a loss. She had introduced me to galactic Reiki which I still use in my practice. But the real magic was in the "honeycomb" she gave me.

We began to incorporate it into our healing sessions for people and animals. It was also included in the attunements of all people and animals. This box of light – this honeycomb –was so powerful and healing physically, mentally and spiritually. It was being given to us by Sammy Diva to help shift the vibration of the planet and to get us all where we need to be.

The honeycomb was healing many people we worked with. Our experience was that it complimented the Reiki energy making it stronger. It flowed faster. And our clients were feeling it, finding it incredibly grounding, centering and appeared to be recalibrating their entire being. Sammy Diva made it known to us that it was a new form of healing and it was available everywhere.

One day, while browsing inside a metaphysical shop and book store with a friend, Sammy Diva's presence was of course with me, I made the most astounding find. My friend was asking for aragonite, and as soon I turned around to look it at, I gasped. *"OMG, honeycomb!"* I could feel its strong vibration when I held it in my hand.

I brought it home with me and sat in meditation with it. Sammy Diva told me it was the physical form of the honeycomb. I used it in our attunements and the honeycomb crystal began to work immediately. For Reiki Fur Babies, things continued to unfold and expand in such amazing new ways.

I noticed people were reaching out to me in response to my blog posts about Sammy Diva and my experiences with her in 5D. It was like a gathering of like-minded people that only Sammy Diva could have brought together. We all had a like-minded soul purpose to help the planet in whatever way were being called to – be it healing or coaching or whatever service we could offer. And behind the scenes, Sammy Diva took care of us all.

I know of several people who were receiving the honeycomb on an almost daily basis and miracles of healing occurred for them. The testimonies were mind blowing. For some people, maybe the honeycomb might seem a bit woo woo. But, for those of us who were being open to receiving and just allowing it, even though it was beyond our realm of reasoning, by not being attached to the how, we could feel it working. And it was just the beginning.

I continued to learn and teach others important lessons in healing such as, always set intentions that are for your highest good and don't be attached to the *how* or the outcome, so that things that are so out of your realm of thinking can come in – MIRACLES!

Like a sudden shift, a year had passed since Sammy Diva transitioned. It had gone by so quickly. That past year had been amazing with all that transpired. If anyone were to have told me these things were going to happen when my yellow Labrador transitioned, I would have not believed them. But, here I am – a witnesses to all the magnificent work her soul showed me and taught me. One of many witnesses, I should say.

Incredible as it sounds, Sammy Diva brought in the healing honeycomb. Reiki Fur Babies' healing took off to a whole new level. We witnessed more miracles that year in the animals and people than ever before. We were honored to partake in the attunements of animals, plants, Archangels, unicorns and places on our planet.

That morning as I contemplated the first anniversary of Sammy Diva's transition, I asked her to send me a sign that she was still around. WHOA! It was partly unexpected and yet completely amazing. I was during a 5D experience when a friend of mine gave me a booster shot. The shot reminded me of getting a flu shot. Later, when I told my friend what she had done, she replied without hesitation, "Yeah. I'll tell you about it later."

It turned out to be what she called a "BEE12Booster" and it was related to Sammy Diva and the honeycomb. It made so much sense that this friend would be the one to come give me the shot. Sammy Diva's healing honeycomb continued to heal the planet and spread! It was very cool. Powerful!

Months went by and many changes were going on with me at home that made me miss Sammy Diva more than ever. I had not felt her near me lately. Grief always comes in waves, so this was another one I had to ride out. I contacted my good friend and animal communicator who also had a strong connection with Sammy Diva to ask if she could chat with Sammy and find out how things were going. I knew if she could talk with her, I would feel comforted.

The conversation went like this:

Sammy comes as woman with long black hair and tall. Mochi is a man who is handsome appearing to be the age around 35-40. He is wearing a uniform. The color is a rich cherry red with gold emblems and accents. He also has blue pants on. He is a Commander. His helmet is under his right arm. He is Sammy's guardian. Mochi and Sammy have a deep friendship – they have known each other for eons. This is a very loving and affectionate friendship. Sammy knows this.

Mochi says hi and sends love. You will always be his favorite one he guards. (His favorite "subject").

Now, by this time, I had known that Sammy Diva was no longer a yellow Lab and that she was a beautiful being with long black hair. I even drew a picture of her years before she came to me as a yellow Lab, not knowing it was her. I realized that I hadn't been able to "see" her as this being because I wanted to see her as my yellow Lab.

Continuing with my friend's conversation with Sammy Diva:

Sammy is on the left with a little smile. She has been stepping back a lot because there are things in play for you that she wants to make sure you have a clear field. So, connection is not "mucked up", not to have too many cooks in the kitchen. The main composer is [your twin flame] Phillip. She wants to take a step back so that he can work his magic without any interference. She is always with you when you need her. Don't call on her for manifestations. She can't answer that call. Her transition is now more complicated...very busy and clustered...she wants to go back to an easy time, so you can hear her. Connect for companionship not guidance. Just to hang out. Make it easy. Then once she's in the communication can get more intense. Keep it light. She is never far from you. It's just that the way she used to come in was too much pressure. She is always around you she says. She always loves you. The answer is "yes" (she won't tell me your question, but she says "yes").

I discovered that there was a very deep love between Sammy and Mochi – twin flames. It is a very deep and loving friendship. Mochi wanted to experience being a female feline so that was her experience with me. After the reading, I had been asking Sammy Diva to hang out with me and I even asked her to show me Mochi. I wanted to

46

meet Mochi and see Mochi as this male being!

Then one night I found myself working in this place where people called it 'the theatre.' I was helping them carry things or move things. There was this guy with me the whole time, well, watching over me. I thought he was one of the bosses. I had spent the whole day with him and at the end of the day he kissed me on the cheek and told me I could work again the next day, to come in at 7:30 a.m., since I liked the mornings. There was lunch served and it was amazing.

There were all kinds of people and no one interacted with me except for that guy. I clearly remember eating the food. It was like organic salads that was being grown. They were absolutely beautiful. I kept on saying "yum" the whole time I was eating. The guy laughed and said, "You are kind of loud when you eat," and I said, "I'm a foodie, I love food." He said, "Wow, great." This was a wonderful 5D experience and confirmation that Sammy Diva and Mochi were twin flames.

Yes, the chronicles continued. Sammy Diva told us about a lake filled with honeycomb. It is a lake where we could go astrally! I began going to this beautiful lake every night. I would see my twin flame, Phillip, there. I would see Sammy Diva there. I would even see some of my friends there. The most amazing thing is that the next day when I would talk with my friends, some of them would remember being there at the same time.

As time went on, I started taking more friends and even Lucy, my Corgi, to the lake. It was truly a beautiful and healing place to go. I decided to take Joe, a dog that I had known for years, to the lake too. Here's the story:

We had a Reiki session for Joe years ago. We gave him an angel at that time which he told us would be *"great."* Joe made us laugh when he asked if the angel ate. After all, Joe wasn't quite sure he wanted to share his food. But, when he realized that angels don't eat, he was cool with the idea.

Then Joe ended up having surgery and we had another Reiki session for him. Reiki energy healing is wonderful for pre and post-surgery of any kind. It speeds up the healing as well as helps the surgery go smoothly.

Later down the line, Joe was diagnosed with adenocarcinoma. He came to me one night and asked to be attuned to Reiki. Then I showed Joe the honeycomb lake. From then on, night after night, Joe and I would visit the lake. I told Joe he could go there himself if he wanted.

One night, I woke up at 4:00 a.m. and thought, "Oh, let me see if Joe wants to go the lake." But when I got to the lake, Joe was already there laying next to the lake!

"Ming, where have you been?" he said smiling.

I wanted Candy to interview Joe on how he felt about his attunement like we do with all our clients. Joe revealed that he had spirit animals visiting him and how he was visiting other places in his mind's eye – the lake!!! It was on this lake that Joe asked me to go visit him in 3D. I was so grateful to Sammy Diva for showing us more on the path of healing.

It was a Thanksgiving Day when my experience with 7D

began. My good friend, who is an animal communicator, and I connected to Sammy Diva that day. That's when Sammy Diva told me we would be moving from 5D to 7D. She said we would help others experience 7D as well. The next day, through guided meditation, my crown chakra was opened to 7D. I have never been the same since.

To document this ascension and all I was seeing and connecting with, I created a Pinterest board. I called it *My Journey to 7D*. You are invited to follow me there if your guided to, at: https://www.pinterest.com/reikifurbabies/. You will be able to see pictures of all the beings I discovered who were working and helping me in that dimension – it was a metaphysical experience that was truly out of this world. Some were with me for a shorter time than others. But others, to this day I still rely and ask for their guidance and protection.

I discovered my dragon, Doremus through the 7D portal. Yes…a DRAGON! And Maximus, a large red dragon. I was also paid a visit by star people which I call the Crystal Spelunkers. They showed me a beautiful amethyst that grew and grew and became brighter and brighter – it seemed to expand into a galaxy. It was such an amazing vision and during that time I was filled with a joy unimaginable.

The Crystal Spelunkers continued to visit me for three more days, showing me what they could do with the amethyst, emeralds, quartz and pink quartz. 7D is a place where all things are possible – where we are open to all things. It is a place where we truly come home to who we truly are.

During my meditations in 7D, I also found an open window where a pod of dolphins came in and I could hear myself feeling delighted. I could feel and touch the dolphins, they were there to raise the vibration. Goddess Inanna appeared with two lionesses to assist in the journey as well as Goddess Brigit. It was a joy beyond expression to work with these wonderful goddesses.

One goddess, Goddess Anoche, appeared to me five times. By the third time her face was completely in mine and she took her hands and put them on my shoulders. I was feeling a charge of electricity going through me as she did this.

There's more. One night the wolf moon brought in a huge celebration. I was at a party, animals were being blessed and given gifts. Fairies were dancing. An older woman came to me and said, "I wanted to tell you how much Sammy Diva has been helping me." I thought to myself, WOW! Everyone at this party was from all dimensions of time.

The Goddess Morrigan was sending me downloads of energy and blessing everyone in my family and my friends. I could hear their names as they were receiving the gifts. I could see Philip clearer and longer and the bond felt so much stronger than ever before. He showed me his cool cell phone and how to text him. I heard *wishes granted!*

Goddess Morrigan first appeared to me a couple of days before Christmas 2015. She was covered under a hooded cloak. I had never heard of her and knew nothing about her, only that she was a misunderstood goddess. She asked if I would work with her. After much consideration I said it would be my honor.

The first night we worked together, Morrigan showed me the stars and asked me to send healing, which I did. Every night was amazing. She showed me her love for the animals and for children. She showed me how to use a quantum healing energy ball to help people heal by going back in time! I tried it several times on people, animals and even myself. It worked, and it was so powerful. It was a gift that I gave to all the Reiki practitioners attuned by Reiki Fur Babies.

Morrigan showed me shape shifting and brought me gifts of sprit animals – a panther named Jade and a white tiger named Jedi – to be my protectors. She also assisted me in healing one of my closest friends. One night we went into a dragon lair and freed hundreds and hundreds and hundreds of dragons – a blue dragon's family. They are now freed!

Astounding as all this may sound, it is all true. My journey with Sammy Diva has been so incredible. I have Sammy Diva to thank for this amazing journey unfolding, a journey that I am so happy to be able to finally write about and share in a book. Because it really does show how connected our souls are, why we have come to be here, sharing experiences with each other. We are all, in some way, shape or form, joining forces to spread healing and love.

If there is one thing I would like for you take away after reading this is, the life of our fur babies after transition does continue – on the other side of Rainbow Bridge – where the soul is eternal, and we can always connect with them. I really hope you can find some consolation in knowing ALL of this.

Conclusion

More on the saying "time heals all wounds." While still grieving the loss of the physical presence of Lucy, I realize that the grief is slowly becoming 'manageable.' That's the best word to describe my feelings when asked how I am doing. The grief is not gone, and I don't think it ever is really gone. But it's manageable. Meaning I can function. I can eat. I can sleep. I'm not tearing up every hour. My heart no longer physically hurts. I can laugh more often. Listening to someone that is happy is not irritating to me anymore.

I am also able to care about someone else's problems one again – because when processing your grief, it's important to recognize you might not have the bandwidth to care for someone that is going through a rough time. You may need to be honest with them and let them know.

If part of your daily life involves going to work, you may have to try your best to put your feelings aside for the day, unfortunately, to do your work. It would be good if your work gave you some time off to grieve. I remember I had a few days to myself when Sammy Diva first transitioned, but I did have to work. With Lucy I had the blessing to be self-employed, so I was more generous with my schedule. But, if you must work and can't take time for yourself, you might just have to wait till you get home to cry. That is okay too.

Also, be gentle with those around you who are also grieving. Lucy had a big fan base. People that I didn't even know very well were grieving her physical departure. Lucy had a job the last few years of her life. She was a greeter at a metaphysical store. She loved it. She was great at it and could even tell if someone was going to buy something in the store. She was so fun to watch. She had her own 'gang' there called the Pineapple Gang, and they named her the Pineapple Princess.

I had to consciously tell myself to allow my friends to grieve their own way. It was difficult for me though, wondering why my close friends were not as seemingly heartbroken as I was. If you find yourself in this situation, try to withhold judgement and recognize if you are angry, that this is just part of the process. In fact, at first it felt as if I was experiencing the grief steps all at once, simultaneously.

I am not hiding from people anymore. I'm already mostly an introvert, but there were times I didn't even want to go out of the house. If you are feeling like that, it's okay. You're still grieving. As my close friends would tell me, "You're doing great!"

Also, if you do have a couple of friends you can lean on, lean on them. Often my friends would just listen to me and that is all I needed. It's consoling to be able to talk about how you are feeling or sometimes just sharing memories and stories of your fur baby.

Another practical thing is, on days I felt good, I took advantage of that while realizing that the next day maybe all I wanted to do was watch movies. So, when that burst of good energy came for the day I would be productive. For instance, I would record some podcasts – because no one wants to listen to me crying on a podcast while I'm trying to be inspirational to my listeners.

As your grief becomes manageable and your vibration rises you will find you are able to tap into your fur baby's energy more, you will see her more. Don't be discouraged if it takes a while. Believe me, it's not that she is not trying. Just be open and look forward to her connecting with you as you become happier and less sad. It's worth it.

Who knows? Perhaps you, too, will find yourself on a brand-new magical journey of love and healing…with your Angel from Rainbow Bridge!

I wish you lots of love and healing.

About the Author

Additional works by Dr. Chee can be found at:
Reiki Fur Babies website: www.reikifurbabies.com
The Money Alchemist website: themoneyalchemist.com.

For daily updates about energy healing, wellbeing, attunements and transition of animals, please follow Reiki Fur Babies on Facebook @ReikiFurBabies.

You may also follow Dr. Chee on social media via Facebook @Money.Alchemist and Instagram handler MoneyAlchemist.

Dr. Chee may also be contacted through email at: Ming@TheMoneyAlchemist.com.